SPECIAL REPORTS

HURRICANE HARVEY

BY CLIFF WATERFORD

CONTENT CONSULTANT
JENNIFER COLLINS
ASSOCIATE PROFESSOR, SCHOOL OF GEOSCIENCES
UNIVERSITY OF SOUTH FLORIDA

Essential Library
An Imprint of Abdo Publishing | abdopublishing.com

abdopublishing.com

Published by Abdo Publishing, a division of ABDO, PO Box 398166, Minneapolis, Minnesota 55439.

Printed in the United States of America, North Mankato, Minnesota
012018
012018

THIS BOOK CONTAINS RECYCLED MATERIALS

Cover Photo: Jay Janner/Austin American-Statesman/AP Images
Interior Photos: Melissa Phillip/Houston Chronicle/AP Images, 4–5; David J. Phillip/AP Images, 9, 51, 52–53; Kim Brent/Beaumont Enterprise/AP Images, 14; NASA, 16–17; Fritz Hasler & Hal Pierce/NASA/GSFC/Science Source, 20; Stephen M. Katz/The Virginian-Pilot/AP Images, 24; Gerald Herbert/AP Images, 27, 37, 59; Alan Diaz/AP Images, 28; Mark Ralston/AFP/Getty Images, 30–31; iStockphoto, 34; Jennifer Reynolds/The Galveston County Daily News/AP Images, 35; Karen Warren/Houston Chronicle/AP Images, 38–39; Jim Olive/Polaris/Newscom, 40–41; Aaron M. Sprecher/AP Images, 43, 54; Xinhua/Sipa USA/Newscom, 47; John Glaser/Cal Sport Media/AP Images, 56; Malcolm McClendon/Polaris/Newscom, 57; Mark Mulligan/Houston Chronicle/AP Images, 60; David Kent/Star-Telegram/AP Images, 64–65; Michael Stravato/Polaris/Newscom, 67; Elizabeth Conley/Houston Chronicle/AP Images, 71; Brett Coomer/Houston Chronicle/AP Images, 78–79; Sepp Friedhuber/iStockphoto, 80–81; KSC/NASA, 83; MOREL/SIMAX/Sipa/AP Images, 84; Andy Newman/AP Images, 86; M. Stan Reaves/Rex Features/AP Images, 89; Bill Clark/CQ Roll Call/AP Images, 90–91; LM Otero/AP Images, 92; Gregory Bull/AP Images, 95; Jay Janner/Austin American-Statesman/AP Images, 98

Editor: Alyssa Krekelberg
Series Designer: Maggie Villaume

Publisher's Cataloging-in-Publication Data

Names: Waterford, Cliff, author.
Title: Hurricane Harvey / by Cliff Waterford.
Description: Minneapolis, Minnesota : Abdo Publishing, 2018. | Series: Special reports
Identifiers: LCCN 2017955913 | ISBN 9781532114007 (lib.bdg.) | ISBN 9781532152900 (ebook)
Subjects: LCSH: Natural disasters--Juvenile literature. | Hurricanes--Juvenile literature. | Disaster relief--Juvenile literature. | Gulf Coast (U.S.)--Juvenile literature.
Classification: DDC 976.044--dc23
LC record available at https://lccn.loc.gov/2017955913

CONTENTS

CHAPTER ONE

A FLOODED CITY

In the early morning hours of August 27, 2017, a thudding sound woke Yvonne Ferguson-Smith. She ran to the bathroom in her wood-frame house. The sound had been her bathroom ceiling collapsing after days of heavy rain. The floor was littered with pieces of damp drywall. Within the next few hours, floodwaters submerged the stairs outside of her home and began to spill into her living room. Ferguson-Smith realized she and her family would have no choice but to leave. The storm surge from Hurricane Harvey was quickly flooding their home.

Two days earlier, the hurricane had made landfall near Corpus Christi, Texas, hundreds of miles southwest of Ferguson-Smith's home in northeastern Houston.

Some Texas residents climbed into rescue boats once the area began to flood.

TUNE-UP

Within the eyewall of the storm, winds churned at 130 miles per hour (209 kmh), uprooting trees and structures in the hurricane's path.[1] The storm lost momentum as it made its way inland, but the strong winds and heavy rains were relentless.

HURRICANE HARVEY'S PATH

Hurricane Harvey first made landfall northeast of Corpus Christi, Texas, on the night of August 25, 2017. In the early morning hours of August 26, the hurricane also hit towns along the northeastern coast of Copano Bay in Texas. These included the towns of Rockport and Fulton. Because they were within the eyewall of the storm, these areas were hit hardest. Then, in the early morning of August 30, the storm hit the coastal town of Cameron, Louisiana, along the Gulf of Mexico. In addition, the storm caused flash floods in other southern states that were not directly hit, including Mississippi, Tennessee, and Arkansas.

Ferguson-Smith's house had been built on low-lying swampland between two bayous. She lived there with her husband, Rico, and their teenage son and daughter. Ferguson-Smith's sister, Charmane, also lived with them. As the storm raged on, rain and marsh water flooded the streets in their neighborhood. They watched as their neighbors evacuated. Families piled into rescue boats. Some people stuffed their belongings into floating dumpsters that they pushed through the high floodwaters.

Ferguson-Smith's son, Travis, pleaded with his parents to leave. He feared snakes floating in the water as the rising tides flushed animals out of their natural habitats. But Charmane was afraid to leave. Neither she nor Ferguson-Smith knew how to swim, and the fast-moving, murky water appeared threatening. Charmane also had schizophrenia, a mental illness that made her more agitated in stressful situations. Ferguson-Smith had another important reason to stay as well. As a nurse at a nearby hospital, she was trained to help people during times of disaster. One morning in the days after the storm first hit, her boss texted her. He asked her to come to the hospital to treat storm victims. Ferguson-Smith surveyed the street outside her home. The floodwaters had risen and

DISPLACED WILDLIFE

Hundreds of thousands of alligators live in Texas, mostly in swampy areas on the southeastern coast of the state. Along with snakes and many other animals, they migrated to higher grounds to escape the floods from Harvey. These animals are often afraid of humans and will not attack unless provoked. Of the 23 snake species in the Houston area, only five are venomous.[2] The animal to be most concerned about during periods of flooding, according to both wildlife officials and residents, is the red imported fire ant. This invasive insect species is known for its painful stings, which can cause blisters, burning, or infections. In clusters, these ants can float on water without drowning. Their bodies produce a type of waterproof wax, and they latch onto one another's legs to keep afloat.

submerged her car. She wouldn't be able to drive. It was too dangerous to leave.

On the morning of August 27, however, Ferguson-Smith and her family had no choice but to evacuate. By then, Harvey had dumped more than a foot (0.3 m) of rain in Houston and other parts of southeastern Texas. The National Weather Service (NWS) had issued a flash flood emergency for the area. Meteorologists for the NWS warned, "Catastrophic flooding in the Houston metropolitan area is expected to worsen and may become historic."[3] In their house, Ferguson-Smith and her family waded through water that had risen past their ankles. Yasmine, Ferguson-Smith's daughter, found a garter snake floating in the water in her bedroom. The family quickly packed backpacks full of supplies. Then, they opened the door and stepped outside into waist-deep water. They carried their backpacks over their heads. Ferguson-Smith kept an eye on her sister, hoping Charmane wouldn't break down from the stress.

"I DON'T THINK I CAN CRY ANYMORE. I'VE GONE THROUGH A LOT OF EMOTIONS—A LOT OF ANGER, SADNESS, YOU KNOW, EVEN ENVY: WHY DIDN'T MY HOUSE MAKE IT?"[4]

— PEGGY BOURG, SURVIVOR

Thousands of vehicles were destroyed by Harvey's floodwaters.

Ferguson-Smith and her family slowly made their way to higher ground, pushing against the current. They managed to reach the parking lot of a nearby store. A crowd of people had gathered there. A massive 18-wheeler rescue truck arrived. Everyone clambered onto the open truck bed, and they were driven to a local church. Once they arrived, they were able to dry off. A city bus pulled up to the church. It transported Ferguson-Smith and her family to the George R. Brown Convention Center in downtown Houston, where they took shelter with thousands of other people who had also been displaced from their homes.

HOUSTON AND HARVEY

In 2017, Houston was the fourth largest city in the United States. It had a population of more than two million people and a population density of approximately 3,500 people per square mile (2.6 sq km).[5] The mayor of Houston, Sylvester Turner, was concerned for the safety of the city's residents. However, he decided against issuing a mandatory evacuation order. Government officials can issue mandatory evacuation orders to urge residents to leave a danger-prone area in the event of a perceived upcoming emergency. The purpose of a mandatory evacuation order is to get people to safety before a hurricane or other type of disaster strikes.

"THIS IS A CITY OF HOPE AND OPPORTUNITY. AND THIS IS A CITY THAT WILL COME BACK STRONGER THAN IT HAS EVER BEEN. OF THAT I HAVE NO DOUBTS."[6]

— HOUSTON MAYOR SYLVESTER TURNER

Houston's mayor had last issued a mandatory evacuation order in late September of 2005. Hurricane Rita, a strong storm that had developed over the Atlantic Ocean, was about to make landfall on the southeastern coast of Texas. Houston was in the path of the storm.

More than three million people attempted to evacuate Houston and the surrounding region. This was the largest mass evacuation in US history at that time. An endless line of cars clogged the main highway out of the city. The traffic jam was more than 100 miles (160 km) long. Cars stalled in the road as they ran out of gas, which made traffic even worse. Passengers sat idle in temperatures of 100 degrees Fahrenheit (38°C), many choosing not to use air conditioning in order to conserve gas. More than 100 people died during this evacuation, some from heat stroke and others from traffic accidents or car fires. Fewer than ten people died from the hurricane itself.[7]

While the evacuation had been intended to save people, it ended up putting many in danger. Turner did not want to repeat that mistake with Harvey. Because there had not been much advance warning about how intense and destructive Harvey could be, the mayor and other government officials did not think there would be time to organize a safer, more effective evacuation effort. But Ed Emmett, a Texas county judge, assured the public that even though a mandatory evacuation wasn't issued, emergency teams would be well prepared to help people

MORE TO THE STORY

VOLUNTARY VS. MANDATORY EVACUATION

Houston was not the only city or town within the hurricane's path that decided not to issue a mandatory evacuation order. Joe McComb, the mayor of Corpus Christi, Texas, issued a voluntary instead of a mandatory evacuation order. Under a voluntary evacuation order, government officials warn the public that an imminent event is potentially life threatening, but officials do not require residents to evacuate. Under a mandatory evacuation order, residents are ordered to leave the area. The government provides rescue services to help evacuate residents. But according to Texas law, if someone decides to leave too late, the resident is required to pay for the cost of the rescue. McComb was aware that requiring emergency workers to try to evacuate unwilling residents would also put many rescue workers in danger. He said about his decision: "It can be a real tug between your heart and your head. We all know we got one goal in mind—keeping people alive."[8]

stay safe during the storm. "When a hurricane comes, you know to get people out of harm's way, you know where the storm surge is going to hit. So we have a very defined process for moving people out of storm surge," he said.[9]

EVACUATION AND POVERTY

Another barrier to evacuation was poverty. In Houston, 22.5 percent of people lived below the poverty line.[10] Since 1980, the number of high-poverty neighborhoods in the area has doubled. African Americans and other people of color within the area were most likely to be affected by poverty and unemployment.

Cars and survival supplies are often needed to evacuate. Some people did not have cars or could not afford public transportation. Some people who did have cars could not afford gas or necessary supplies.

In addition, many did not have home insurance, or else their insurance plans did not cover flood damage. Some stayed to try to protect their homes. Others stayed to protect their families or provide assistance to people. Hundreds of people volunteered for rescue missions and relief efforts. Emmett and other government officials

Many people who were caught in the storm were forced to seek shelter.

"WITH ANY NATURAL DISASTER THERE'S GOING TO BE ANGER AND SADNESS, BUT AT THE SAME TIME THERE'S HAPPINESS THAT PEOPLE WERE LEFT WITH THEIR LIVES. THEY MAY HAVE LOST EVERYTHING BUT THEY STILL HAVE THEIR FAMILY."[11]

— SHANE SINGLETON, SURVIVOR AND VOLUNTEER RESCUER

asked people with boats and water vehicles to volunteer for rescue efforts.

While Ferguson-Smith and her family took refuge in a convention center, more than 30,000 other displaced people also found safe shelters throughout Texas.[12] Convention centers, sports arenas, and churches opened their doors to people in need. Ferguson-Smith and her family slept on cots and stocked up on food provided by volunteers. They read donated books and magazines as they waited out the storm.

Harvey finally died out around August 31. After roads cleared and floodwaters receded, people began venturing back to their homes to assess the damage. Ferguson-Smith and her family visited their home. They were hit by the smell of mold when they stepped inside. Water damage was visible in every room. Restoring their home and their lives would take a lot of work. But after everything they had survived, they knew they would be up to the task.

A HEROIC RESCUE

When flash floods from Harvey hit Houston in late August 2017, many people were still in their homes. Andrea Smith and her husband, Greg, were trapped in their apartment along with Greg's mother in the early morning of August 28. Andrea was pregnant and had started going into labor. Greg and his mother tried to call 911 and the US Coast Guard, but their calls wouldn't go through. Luckily, one of their neighbors got through to a friend whose father lived near a fire station. He alerted the firefighters to the situation. Soon, a dump truck full of firefighters had pulled up to the apartment. Andrea and Greg's neighbors waded out into the waist-high floodwaters and formed a human chain. They guided the couple to the truck, and the truck drove to a nearby hospital. Andrea later gave birth to a baby girl.

CHAPTER TWO

HOW A HURRICANE FORMS

A tropical cyclone is a generic term for a low-pressure system that forms over tropical or subtropical waters. It has an organized convection and a closed circulation. In the Northern Hemisphere, tropical cyclones spin counterclockwise. In the Southern Hemisphere, they spin clockwise. The Earth's rotation causes this difference. A tropical cyclone with high wind speeds is called a hurricane in the North Atlantic or eastern North Pacific. In other parts of the world these storms are not called hurricanes but have regionally specific names. For example, in the Northwest Pacific they are known as typhoons.

A NASA satellite captured an image of Harvey as it hit Texas.

CORIOLIS EFFECT

The Coriolis effect explains why hurricanes north of the equator spin the opposite direction of those south of the equator. Earth rotates, which deflects air so that it does not move in a straight path as it travels from high-pressure areas to low-pressure areas. Air is deflected to the right in the Northern Hemisphere and to the left in the Southern Hemisphere. Hurricanes spin in the direction the air is being deflected in either hemisphere.

Regardless of their name, they are the most destructive of all storms. Hurricane season officially begins in June and ends in November in the North Atlantic. August through October is the peak of the season.

Dozens of tropical waves emerge off Africa every year. The tropical waves that encounter favorable conditions have the potential to form into tropical storms and hurricanes. These conditions include warm waters, moist air, and low wind shear. Some of the waves develop into tropical disturbances. These are small areas of thunderstorms. If this area of thunderstorms develops a distinct counterclockwise circulation around the low-pressure center, it becomes a tropical depression. Even though tropical depressions have well-defined circulation associated with them, the low-pressure center isn't low enough to cause strong winds. When the air pressure associated with tropical depressions becomes even lower, and wind speeds increase to at least 39 miles per hour (63 kmh), the tropical depression becomes a tropical storm. When the pressure decreases even more, to the extent that winds reach or exceed 74 miles per hour (119 kmh), it becomes a hurricane.[1]

STRUCTURE OF A HURRICANE

A hurricane has three basic parts: the outer region, the eyewall, and the eye at the center. The outer region begins about 20 miles (30 km) from the center of the storm and continues to a radius of 100 miles (160 km) or more.[2] This region is layered with rings of rain bands. Heavy rainfall and strong winds occur within the rain bands. The closer the bands are to the center, the stronger the winds.

NAMING HURRICANES

When a storm becomes a tropical storm, it is given a name. This is to avoid confusion if there are two storms at once. The storm keeps the name if it becomes a hurricane. This means that Hurricane Harvey began as Tropical Storm Harvey. Hurricanes in the Atlantic follow six lists of names that alternate between male and female names from A to W. One list is used each year. After six years, naming starts back with the first list. So the list used in 2018 will be reused in 2024. If more hurricanes happen in a year than there are names on that year's list, the hurricanes take Greek alphabet names. If a hurricane is particularly destructive, its name is retired. A new name will take its place in the list. Retired names include Katrina, Ike, Irene, and Sandy.

The second part of a hurricane is the eyewall. The eyewall begins about 10 miles (15 km) from the center of the storm and has a radius of 20 miles (30 km).[3] This is the most destructive part of a hurricane. It has the storm's strongest winds and heaviest rains. Clouds are densest here, starting low to the ground and rising higher than clouds in the outer region.

The third part, the eye, is the center of the hurricane. It is the low-pressure center around which the storm rotates. The air in the eye is warm and skies are often clear.

The eye of a hurricane is the calmest part of the storm.

DAMAGING EFFECTS

Hurricanes are incredibly powerful, destructive forces. They can cause damage in many ways. Storm surges happen along coastal regions. Low air pressure over the water raises the height of the water slightly. In addition, the strong winds in and near the eyewall have more of an impact as they blow ocean water into a surge. When the hurricane blows the storm surge onto a coastline, it can cause serious flooding, even miles inland. Flooding from storm surges is typically the deadliest threat of a hurricane. In addition, large, strong waves that come with a storm surge damage homes and coastlines.

DEADLY STORM SURGE

In 1970, a tropical cyclone called the Bhola Cyclone hit what is now Bangladesh. The storm surge was estimated to be as high as 30 feet (9 m) tall. It killed more than 300,000 people. Nearly one-half of the city of Tazumuddin's population perished.[4] It is the deadliest tropical cyclone on record.

"I LOOKED OUT AND THE NEXT THING YOU KNOW, THE WATER JUST CAME UP THROUGH THE GRATES. IT CAME UP SO QUICKLY YOU COULDN'T DO ANYTHING ABOUT IT. IF YOU WANTED TO MOVE YOUR CAR TO HIGHER GROUND YOU DIDN'T HAVE ENOUGH TIME."[5]

—LEO QUIGLEY OF LITTLE FERRY, NEW JERSEY, DESCRIBING HOW QUICKLY HURRICANE SANDY BEGAN FLOODING THE TOWN IN 2012

Heavy rains also cause flooding. Watersheds, which are regions of land where water collects and drains into a waterway, can handle average amounts of rain. But in heavy rains, the waterway may flood. Even when the rain stops, the flooding can remain for days. That is because land developed for human purposes, such as residential use, loses much of its ability to absorb water. This is because natural soil is covered with pavement and buildings. This water will eventually run off into rivers or bodies of water that may already be high from rainfall. The water can crest the banks and flood areas nearby, damaging buildings and ecosystems.

Hurricanes also bring destructive winds. Depending on the hurricane's strength, winds can blow at more than 157 miles per hour (253 kmh).[6] The winds can cause large areas to lose electricity by blowing over power poles. Winds can destroy homes and hurl smaller objects such as street signs into cars or through windows. The outer rain bands of a hurricane, especially to the front and right of the eye in relation to the storm's path, can also form tornadoes. Tornadoes affect a much smaller area than the hurricane's other effects, but they can still be destructive and deadly.

HURRICANE CATEGORIES

Scientists use a scale called the Saffir-Simpson Hurricane Wind Scale to classify just how powerful and destructive a given hurricane is. The scale breaks hurricanes into five categories. Category 1 is the weakest of hurricanes. It has winds between 74 and 95 miles per hour (119 and 153 kmh).[7] These hurricanes will damage plant life and mobile homes but generally not anchored buildings.

Category 2 hurricanes have winds between 96 and 110 miles per hour (154 and 177 kmh).[8] These hurricanes will blow some trees down, damage roofs, and break windows. The wind will also cause widespread power outages.

SAFFIR-SIMPSON HURRICANE WIND SCALE

Herbert Seymour Saffir and Robert H. Simpson created the Saffir-Simpson Hurricane Wind Scale in 1975. It originally listed potential wind destruction and storm surge threats as well as the central pressure of a storm. In the 1990s, central pressure information was removed from the scale and replaced by direct wind measurements. In 2010, scientists cut the storm surge from the scale because that element is not always linked with a hurricane's wind. For example, a Category 2 hurricane may create a much higher storm surge than a Category 4.

Category 3 hurricane winds blow at between 111 and 129 miles per hour (178 and 208 kmh).[9] These hurricanes can rip open walls on smaller buildings and homes, knock down big trees, and strip plants of their leaves. They will destroy mobile homes. Power and running water will be out for days or weeks. Category 3 or higher hurricanes are known as major hurricanes.

Category 4 hurricanes have winds ranging from 130 to 156 miles per hour (209 to 251 kmh).[10] All signs are blown down, and homes and small buildings may lose walls or roofs. Power could be out for months, and the area will be unlivable while repairs are made.

Category 5 hurricanes are the strongest storms. Winds are stronger than 157 miles per hour (253 kmh).[11] The storm will completely level some buildings and homes and strip walls and roofs off of others. The area may be unlivable for months.

TRACKING HURRICANES

The extensive damage that hurricanes can cause makes tracking them very important. Predicting when and where a hurricane will hit can help people prepare

Approximately one month after Harvey, Hurricane Maria hit Puerto Rico as a Category 4 hurricane.

buildings for the storm and can also save lives. Scientists have several ways to track a hurricane. Satellites are the most important tool for catching a hurricane early in its formation. Scientists can use satellite images to find where a hurricane is forming and then track its growth and path.

Once a hurricane moves closer to shore, scientists can use Doppler radar to track the storm. Doppler radar sends out radio waves from an antenna. When the waves hit things such as rain drops in the air, they bounce back to the radar. The amount of energy that bounces back to the radar and the time it takes for that energy to bounce back indicates the distance of a storm. Scientists can use Doppler radar to investigate hurricanes hundreds of miles away from the radar station. Doppler

TIROS

The Television Infrared Observation Satellite 1 (TIROS-1) was the first US weather satellite. It launched on April 1, 1960, and ran for weeks. NASA used the satellite to test the use of instruments in space. TIROS-1 collected data and helped scientists make accurate weather predictions. It also sent thousands of pictures of Earth's cloud cover back to Earth, allowing researchers to learn more about cloud structure. NASA launched nine more TIROS satellites in the 1960s. These satellites continued to test instruments to prepare for long-term weather satellites. Today, satellites can not only monitor water vapor concentrations in the atmosphere and the warmth or coolness of objects, but they can also alert scientists to damaging radiation from the sun.

The aircraft used to study hurricanes have chutes that drop buoys.

radar can be used to estimate total rainfall and to track a hurricane's movements.

Another way people track hurricanes is by flying straight into them. Hurricane Hunters from the US

Air Force and the National Oceanic and Atmospheric Administration (NOAA) fly around hurricanes and through them into the eyes. They measure weather elements such as wind speeds and air pressure to understand the storm's structure. One instrument they use is a dropsonde. They drop this device from the aircraft. A parachute slows its fall so it can collect information about air pressure, humidity,

Lieutenant Commander Nathan Kahn flies into hurricanes to collect data about the storms.

and temperature. The dropsonde uses radio signals to send the information back to the aircraft.

Another way scientists measure hurricanes is through data buoys. Buoys across the Gulf of Mexico and the coasts collect information on wind speeds, water and air temperatures, and air pressure. The data collected by these methods are used in computer models that help forecast the storm's course and intensity. This information allows people to prepare for a hurricane and evacuate if necessary. These precautions can save lives and reduce damage when a hurricane hits.

"EVERY STORM COMES UP WITH A SURPRISE."[12]

— BILL READ, NATIONAL HURRICANE CENTER DIRECTOR, ON HOW SCIENTISTS CANNOT FORECAST EVERYTHING ABOUT A HURRICANE

HARVEY'S ARRIVAL

In early August 2017, a wave emerged off the western African coast. On August 17, east of the Lesser Antilles in the Caribbean, the disturbance had strengthened to a tropical storm and was given the name Harvey. Harvey continued its westward track and the humidity within the storm dropped, causing Harvey to dissipate. Warnings for the storm ceased.

But then the remnants of the storm reached the Gulf of Mexico on August 23. The warm water there quickly refueled the storm and Harvey strengthened to a tropical depression. Within hours, Harvey was forming an eye. Harvey hit a particularly warm patch of Gulf waters, and on August 25 it grew from a Category 1 to a Category 4 hurricane. After it reached Category 4, it hit

Strong waves and winds hit the Texas coast as Harvey approached on August 25.

Rockport, Texas. Its winds were blowing at 130 miles per hour (209 kmh).[1] Harvey hovered over southern Texas until August 30. It stayed in place so long because its movement was blocked by two high-pressure systems on its southwestern and southeastern sides. This near halt in the storm's movement allowed the storm to cause great destruction in southern Texas.

HURRICANE KATRINA FORMATION

In 2005, the devastating Hurricane Katrina formed in a similar way to Harvey. Katrina hit Florida as a Category 1 hurricane, crossed the state, and moved into the Gulf of Mexico. There, warm waters fueled the hurricane for three days and it became a Category 5 hurricane. Katrina had weakened to a Category 3 hurricane when it hit Louisiana's coast. Katrina caused billions of dollars in damage. Some levees and seawalls that held back rivers, lakes, and the ocean broke or were overtopped, causing drastic flooding. The damage in New Orleans, Louisiana, was especially bad. People who had stayed home had to flee to their rooftops to escape the flooding. Nearly 2,000 people died because of Katrina.

HARVEY'S DESTRUCTIVE POWER

Harvey was the first Category 3 hurricane or higher to hit the United States since 2005. When it hit land, Port Aransas, Texas, reported 132-mile-per-hour (212 kmh) gusts.[2] Harvey knocked out many storm-measuring stations before experts could measure the strongest parts of the hurricane. In Rockport

MORE TO THE STORY

PREPARING FOR HARVEY

As Harvey approached the US coast, people prepared for the storm. A few county officials instructed residents to evacuate immediately because rescuers might not be able to reach them once the storm hit. People who did not evacuate or who lived in areas without a mandatory evacuation purchased medications, first aid supplies, food, water, and pet supplies to last several days. They had flashlights and cash, and they packed up vehicles with clothes and emergency supplies in case they needed to leave. Some cleared their gutters to make sure they could handle the rain and prevent flooding in homes. Many people nailed boards over their windows to prevent the glass from breaking.

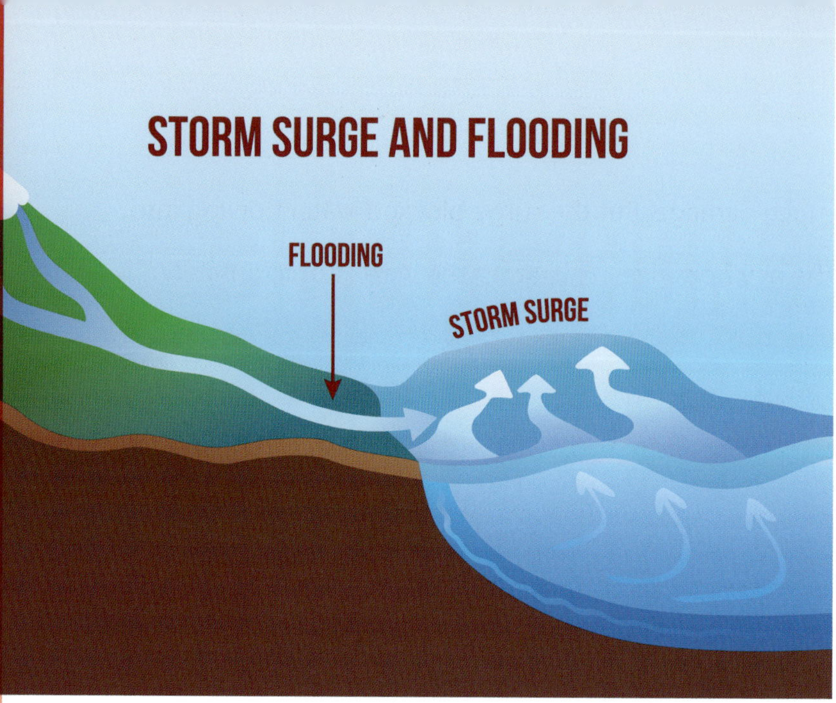

A storm surge creates a large rise in water. If the surge blocks another body of water, such as a river, water will back up and cause flooding.

and Fulton, Texas, the winds blew roofs off and collapsed walls. They pushed down trees and power poles. The cities lost power and running water.

The storm surge when Harvey hit land was not especially high. Hurricane Katrina in 2005 had a much larger and more devastating surge. Across much of the southern Texas coast, the storm surge for Harvey was between 3 and 6 feet (1 and 1.8 m). Harvey's highest surge was 12 feet (3.7 m) above the normal sea level at Arkansas Wildlife Refuge.[3] The surge also led to high waters in Galveston Bay, where Houston lies. The sea level had only risen by 3 feet (1 m), which alone wouldn't have done much damage. But the surge blocked water flowing into the bay from rivers, piling up the water approximately 9 feet (2.7 m).[4] With the surge overflowing the bay, the rainwater Harvey brought had nowhere to drain.

"THIS WILL BE A DEVASTATING DISASTER, PROBABLY THE WORST DISASTER THE STATE'S SEEN."[6]

— WILLIAM LONG, FEDERAL EMERGENCY MANAGEMENT AGENCY ADMINISTRATOR, PREDICTING HARVEY'S SIGNIFICANCE TWO DAYS AFTER IT HIT LAND

When Harvey hit land, its winds were strong and its surges did damage, but Harvey weakened to a tropical storm the day after, on August 26. Heavy rains, along with the lack of forward motion, were responsible for the immense damage Harvey caused.

For several days, Harvey stalled out over southeastern Texas and Louisiana, dropping 40 inches (102 cm) of rain in some areas.[5] An area of almost 29,000 square

During Harvey, some people videotaped the storm surge.

miles (75,000 sq km) received at least 20 inches (51 cm) of rain.[7] This torrent of rain led to widespread flooding. With nowhere to go, vast areas of floodwaters acted like a warm ocean. Harvey sucked the moisture back up and rained it down again for days. People became stranded in their flooded homes. Houston residents scrambled to escape. People with boats helped their neighbors evacuate.

SAVING LIVES

In 2016, Houston resident Nick Sissa bought a military truck on impulse at an auction. He wasn't quite sure why. But when Harvey struck, he knew what he needed to do. He set out in his truck to work with the Houston Fire Department. For three days, he drove through flooded streets and heavy rain, picking up stranded residents and driving them to safety. During shifts lasting eight hours or longer, he rescued hundreds of people.

People formed human chains to rescue others from stranded cars. Convention centers and even furniture stores became emergency shelters. Two Texas cities beat the record of rainfall for a hurricane. Nederland received 60.58 inches (153.87 cm). Groves received 60.54 inches (153.77 cm).[8] On top of all the rain, Harvey also produced tornadoes in other southern states.

Finally, on August 30, Harvey began moving a bit and reached southwestern and central Louisiana. It weakened to a tropical depression but still caused flooding in the state. The next day, the system dissipated and the National Hurricane Center stopped issuing advisories. But it left behind a disaster. Cities were left to begin the long task of rebuilding their neighborhoods and businesses.

Rescue workers helped stranded Texas residents flee the floodwaters.

FROM THE HEADLINES

PETS SHELTERED FROM HARVEY

In 2005, many people were forced to leave their pets behind in order to escape Hurricane Katrina. Most emergency shelters did not allow pets. Evacuation crews would often only allow people on rescue craft. Other people remained in their homes with their pets. Some owners and many pets lost their lives in the storm. Overall, more than 100,000 pets were left behind in Katrina, and 70,000 died.[9] Americans were saddened and angered by images of dogs stranded on rooftops with floodwaters all around.

When Harvey arrived, pet owners in Houston chose to stay outside of emergency centers so they could care for their pets. These owners were willing to face the storm so their pets wouldn't be abandoned. Upon seeing this, city officials quickly stepped in. Katrina had taught everyone a lesson. Pets would officially be allowed in Houston evacuation centers. Many other centers around Texas either allowed pets or arranged separate housing. And rescue centers accepted dogs, cats, and even pet pigs.

Seven-year-old Reniah Knight of Houston clutched her dog, Buster, after Harvey passed.

CHAPTER FOUR

DESTRUCTION IN HOUSTON

As Harvey moved along the southeastern coast of Texas, it encountered the city of Houston. When combined with its suburbs, the metropolitan area encompasses a region larger than the state of New Jersey, with a population of nearly 6 million.[1] Houston residents are no strangers to storms and floods. The southeastern area of Texas bordering the Gulf of Mexico is frequently hit by the many tropical storms and hurricanes that form. In some cases, these storms cause significant flooding, such as during Tropical Storm Allison in 2001 and Hurricane Ike in 2008.

Piles of trash littered Houston roads after Harvey.

ROAD
WORK
AHEAD

"FLAT-AS-A-PANCAKE"

No amount of planning and engineering can make a city completely safe from natural disasters such as flooding, but the location and layout of Houston actually make it particularly susceptible to a disaster. In order to give the city access to the Gulf of Mexico's shipping lanes, it had to be built on a floodplain along the coast that was naturally prone to flooding. In addition, the area's compact, clay-based soil absorbs little water, and the terrain, which reporter Kim McGuire of the *Houston Chronicle* described as "flat-as-a-pancake," does not allow water to run off easily.[2] As a result, rainwater collects and causes flooding.

AMERICA'S FLOOD CAPITAL

In the past few decades, more people have died from flood-related causes in Texas than in any other state in the United States. Houston alone averages five days of flash floods each year and has experienced several major flooding events in the last 180 years. Its reputation has earned it the nickname America's flood capital.

Houston's population increased significantly in the 1990s and early 2000s as the thriving oil and shipping industries created new jobs. The city had few zoning

Houston has the largest population of any city in the southern United States.

codes to regulate the size and placement of buildings and how land was utilized, so the city expanded at an unprecedented rate. The surrounding prairies and wetlands, which were important for helping store water runoff and releasing it into the Gulf of Mexico, were developed and paved over. Houses and businesses were also built close together to maximize the city's density, leaving little room for water to drain naturally. This urban

"WHAT WAS ONCE FARM OR WETLANDS IS NOW PAVEMENT AND SUBURBIA."[3]

— MATT LANZA, HOUSTON-BASED METEOROLOGIST

sprawl made water management extremely difficult. In addition, maps of flood zones became out of date or were ignored, and homes were built in areas at high risk for flooding. Houston was a disaster waiting to happen.

HOUSTON FLOODS

Houston has an elaborate system to manage storm water, run by the city's Storm Water Maintenance Branch. It includes approximately 3,800 miles (6,100 km) of storm sewer lines with 6,305 exit points, 2,400 miles (3,900 km) of roadside ditches, and 74 miles (119 km) of drainage channels.[4] They funnel water into the San Jacinto River, Buffalo Bayou, and various smaller rivers, creeks, lakes, and bayous, where it slowly drains into the Gulf of Mexico. The edges of some rivers and bayous are lined with concrete to help improve water flow. Storm water is also funneled into man-made structures such as the Addicks

A 500-YEAR FLOOD

The flooding in Houston during Hurricane Harvey was called a 500-year flood. A common misconception is that a 500-year event, such as a major storm or flood, will only happen once in 500 years. It actually refers to an event that has a 1-in-500, or 0.2 percent, chance of occurring in a given year.[5] These events are rare, but they can happen at any time.

and Barker Reservoirs, along with smaller storm water retention ponds that slowly drain water into the ground and channel it into bayous. But much of Houston's storm water infrastructure was built in the 1930s and 1940s and hadn't been sufficiently upgraded as the city expanded over time. In 2017, Stephen Costello, an official with the city of Houston, stated that "over 60 percent of our infrastructure is beyond its useful life."[6] It was not adequate to handle the sort of rainfall seen during Harvey and contributed to the massive flooding in the city.

"HOUSTON IS NOT DESIGNED TO HANDLE THIS KIND OF RAINFALL."[7]

— PROFESSOR SAMUEL BRODY, TEXAS A&M UNIVERSITY

On Sunday, August 27, water in the streets of Houston began to rise as rain from Harvey overwhelmed the city's drainage system and had nowhere else to go. City officials issued flash flood warnings. There was no official order to evacuate, but as the water rose, Houston residents began evacuating their homes on their own. Thousands of people packed what belongings they could and went into the streets. Some drove and others walked, sometimes through knee-deep water. People carried children and pets in their arms above the water. Pets were also placed in inflatable inner tubes, ice chests, and anything else that floated. Evacuees headed to police and fire stations and rescue centers throughout the city.

Over the course of four days, Harvey dumped more than 3 feet (1 m) of rain on the city, totaling approximately 20 trillion gallons (75.7 trillion L) of water.[8] Houston's bayous overflowed, creating widespread flooding. Water rose as high as 20 feet (6 m) in some areas.[9] Many people were trapped in their homes and in their vehicles. According to one reporter, "Floods quickly devoured roads, turned highways into rivers leaving them impassable and trapping unsuspecting motorists."[10] In addition to flooding, high winds blew the roofs off buildings, downed trees and power lines, and turned debris into dangerous projectiles.

RELIGIOUS CENTERS OPEN THEIR DOORS

As people began evacuating their homes, many religious communities opened their doors to evacuees. Christian churches, Jewish synagogues, Islamic mosques, and other places of worship were turned into shelters for people of all faiths. Many provided food, water, and blankets. Rescue workers were also allowed to use these spaces as places to rest.

Rescue workers searched areas around Houston to help people in need of assistance.

BPOA MEETING
AUG 14 630 PM
PARKWAY PLACE

When the storm was over, hundreds of thousands of homes in Houston were damaged or destroyed. Thousands of businesses were damaged. The streets were littered with debris and thousands of abandoned vehicles. The total cost of damages in the city was estimated at close to $90 billion.[11] The storm displaced more than 32,000 people in Houston, left 38 dead in the city, and injured many more.[12]

Seeing the situation unfold, regular citizens began helping others in need, often putting their own lives at risk. Some people who owned boats used them to rescue people who were stranded on the roofs of houses and cars because of the floodwaters. Rescuers used fishing boats, canoes, jet skis, and kayaks, communicating with each other through social media. To help coordinate volunteer rescue operations, Houston resident Keri Henry turned the living room of her home into a makeshift command center, where she used her cell phone and laptop to connect rescuers with those in need. Three friends, Matthew Marchetti, Nate Larson, and Oliver Carter, created a website called Houston Harvey Rescue, where stranded people could pinpoint their locations on a map.

As word of the situation in Houston spread, people from the surrounding area and other states came to help. Many brought boats, including members of Louisiana's famous Cajun Navy. So many people came that some were turned away. Authorities didn't want a large number of civilians to enter a disaster area and run the risk of being injured or killed. In fact, some volunteer rescuers did end up needing to be rescued themselves. And while Houston suffered major damage, it wasn't the only area impacted by Harvey. Southeast Texas and other southern states were hit by the hurricane's destructive power as well.

THE CAJUN NAVY

The Cajun Navy is the informal name of a collection of civilian boat owners throughout southern Louisiana who volunteer their time and watercrafts doing search-and-rescue operations. It was born from an impromptu gathering of people with fishing boats and other small vessels who helped rescue and relief efforts during Hurricane Katrina. They were later dubbed the Cajun Navy after the Cajun people of southern Louisiana. Over time, the group grew to include hundreds of members and divided into several distinct organizations such as Louisiana Cajun Navy and the nonprofit Cajun Navy Relief and Rescue, although they are still collectively known as the Cajun Navy. When Harvey hit Southeast Texas, hundreds of members with boats came to help. They are credited with performing hundreds of rescues in Texas.

FROM THE HEADLINES

A BREACH IN THE BAYOU

In the 1940s, the Army Corp of Engineers built two reservoirs to hold storm water from Houston and the surrounding area. The reservoirs were meant to help prevent flooding. The Addicks and Barker Reservoirs were built in undeveloped prairie lands 20 miles (32 km) west of the city.[13] But by 2017, the metropolitan area had spread to their embankments. A highway was even built between them. Some residents were warned of the potential dangers of living along the reservoirs. Some were not. Many believed the reservoirs couldn't possibly overflow.

On August 27, rainwater began edging towards the top of the 108-foot (33 m) walls of the Addicks Reservoir.[14] To prevent water from overflowing and to make room for additional rainfall, officials from the Army Corps of Engineers decided to release water from the reservoirs into the nearby Buffalo Bayou. This would normally be done slowly over the course of several months, but conditions forced officials to release more water than normal. Despite this measure, water began to spill over the top of the reservoir the

Some residents near the Addicks and Barker Reservoirs retrieved what was left of their possessions. Many people wore masks to protect themselves from breathing in mold.

following day and authorities were forced to increase the rate of discharge. As a result, the Buffalo Bayou overflowed its banks and flooded the surrounding area. Thousands of homes and businesses previously untouched by storm-related flooding were now underwater.

CHAPTER FIVE

HARVEY'S IMPACT

Though Houston has become synonymous with Hurricane Harvey, the storm affected much of Southeast Texas as well as parts of Alabama, Arkansas, Florida, Kentucky, Louisiana, Mississippi, and Tennessee. Cities in these areas saw minor to moderate flooding that shut down numerous streets and highways and delayed and canceled flights from several airports. Strong winds also blew down trees and power lines and spawned dozens of tornadoes.

While wind and rain were directly responsible for much of the damage caused by Harvey, the storm also caused significant damage indirectly. For instance, a Houston oil refinery damaged by the storm leaked hazardous chemicals into the air that formed a toxic

After Harvey, many people had to wait weeks or longer before construction could begin on their homes.

5334

Damage to oil refinery tanks was a serious threat in Texas.

cloud and became a potential health risk. Storm damage at a Houston toxic waste disposal site caused chemicals to leak into the floodwaters, which contaminated land and water for miles. When floodwaters knocked out the power generators at the Arkema chemical plant in Crosby, Texas, its refrigeration units went off-line, causing combustible chemicals to ignite. The toxic smoke emitted by the flames sent first responders to the hospital. Floodwaters also spread toxic chemicals from several Superfund sites. These sites are contaminated areas being cleaned up under the government's Superfund program.

Floodwaters contaminated thousands of homes and commercial buildings. Tons of contaminated food had to be destroyed, and tons more that spoiled due to lack of refrigeration had to be discarded. As floodwaters receded, mold that could make people sick grew on walls and furniture. The countless pools of standing water left in the hurricane's wake had the potential to become breeding grounds for mosquitoes, some of which could carry West Nile and Zika viruses. Flooding also caused sinkholes to form, which damaged streets and highways and blocked traffic. Strong winds blew down numerous power lines, which became electrical hazards.

RESCUE EFFORTS

Police, fire, and medical teams were prepared in advance of the hurricane. In addition to city, county, and state authorities, hundreds of members of the Texas National Guard had been activated and placed at key locations throughout the region. When emergency personnel started receiving calls for help, these rescue teams sprang into action, helping thousands of people evacuate to shelters and assisting those who were injured or stranded. In some areas, rescue teams did house-to-house searches looking for stranded citizens. But as weather conditions worsened, the number of people needing assistance

Texas officers were kept busy during rescue operations.

increased dramatically. At the height of the storm, Houston emergency dispatchers received as many as 900 calls an hour.[1] With call centers backed up and numerous phone lines down, Houston residents used smartphones and devices with wireless Internet to ask for help over social media.

Local rescue forces weren't able to keep up with the cries for help, and some, like Yvonne Ferguson-Smith, were trapped themselves and unable to offer assistance until conditions improved. Authorities had to prioritize the most important calls and requested that only those whose lives were in imminent danger call for help. To assist local forces, the US Coast Guard, Navy, and Air Force were called in, and the contingent of National Guard personnel was increased to 3,000. Eventually the Texas National Guard's entire

The Texas National Guard loaded people into trucks to save them from the floodwaters.

force of 12,000 men and women was activated, and more people were requested from surrounding states to help.[2]

Rescue and evacuation efforts didn't end when the storm was over. It took weeks for the floodwaters to fully recede, during which time some people were still stranded in their homes. Many homes remained without electricity and running water, leaving people without a source of clean drinking water and no way to keep food refrigerated. The Department of Public Safety reported that more than 122,000 people and 5,000 pets were evacuated or rescued after the storm.[3]

Evacuating people from their homes was difficult, but evacuating an entire hospital was a major undertaking with its own unique set of challenges. On August 31, floodwaters caused the city water system in Beaumont, Texas, to fail, leaving businesses and homes without running water. Staff at the Baptist Hospitals of Southeast Texas decided to evacuate nearly 200 patients to other facilities.[4] It took two days to transport the sick and injured to hospitals in Houston. This was accomplished using ambulances, helicopters, and specialized medical buses

Many nursing home residents were evacuated after the storm.

capable of carrying more than a dozen people. Patients had to be moved without causing harm or suffering. Some were transported in beds and gurneys, and some had to be accompanied by medical equipment such as oxygen tanks and dialysis machines.

LOOTERS

Some people saw the confusion and panic brought on by Harvey as an opportunity to loot abandoned homes, vehicles, and businesses. Stores selling jewelry, alcohol, electronics, and firearms were especially singled out by thieves. Looters entered stores and homes by smashing windows and doors. Some gained entry into houses by impersonating Homeland Security agents, which prompted police to warn residents to ask emergency personnel for credentials if they acted suspiciously. But not all break-ins were committed with criminal intent. In some cases, people broke into grocery stores simply to find food and water for themselves and their families.

Responding to criminal complaints took police officers away from rescue operations. Authorities broadcasted a warning that under Texas law stricter penalties were

People made threats to keep looters away from their homes and businesses.

imposed on crimes committed in disaster zones, which could include life in prison. Some citizens took precautions to prevent looting. Some homeowners put signs on their doors and windows stating that intruders would be shot.

Looting continued even after the storm was over. Some of the wet furniture and personal belongings people removed from their homes and set outside to dry were stolen. In the end, police were only able to arrest a handful of looters. Their resources were simply stretched too thin, and the confusion caused by the storm made it difficult to identify looters and easy for them to escape.

DAYS AFTER HARVEY

In the days following the storm, Harvey's devastating effects on the nation came into focus. Eighty-eight people were dead and many more were injured.[5] Hundreds of thousands of homes were damaged or destroyed, and thousands more were without power and water. As many as one million people and thousands of pets were displaced from their homes.

Harvey also had long-reaching impacts on city, state, and national economies. In the countryside, flooding drowned cattle, contaminated animal feed and water supplies, and ruined crops, which hindered the ability of ranchers and farmers to provide food for themselves and others. In cities, tons of commercial goods were damaged or destroyed. Businesses lost income, and the decreased output caused by damaged or powerless manufacturing equipment affected companies throughout the country and around the world that depended on goods made in the storm-ravaged areas. Damaged and backed-up highways, rail lines, airports, and shipping docks prevented commercial goods from entering or leaving cities. Some distributors that were operational put commercial shipping on hold in favor of transporting goods for relief and reconstruction efforts.

EFFECTS ON OIL

The oil industry was especially hit hard by Harvey. A large number of the nation's oil refineries are located in Texas and Louisiana. Numerous refineries and offshore oil rigs were evacuated before the storm. Several refineries and pipelines were damaged during the storm and had to be shut down, resulting in the loss of production of millions of barrels of oil. As a result, 500,000 barrels of oil had to be taken from the US Strategic Petroleum Reserves in an effort to prevent the inflation of gas prices. Still, the hurricane caused the price of gas to go up by an average of 10 cents per gallon (3.8 L) nationwide.[6]

Harvey affected people's lives in many ways. Floodwaters prevented many people from returning to their homes and forced them to live in crowded shelters for days. Not knowing the fate of their homes caused displaced residents considerable stress and anxiety. When they were finally able to return, some found their homes and belongings damaged or destroyed. Some people lost businesses. Others lost family, friends, or pets. Many faced financial difficulties after the storm as they attempted to rebuild their lives. Rescue personnel were under significant stress during the storm due to the constant danger and lack of sleep, while also worrying about the state of their own families and homes. Conditions such as these can lead to post-traumatic stress disorder, with symptoms such as depression, flashbacks, trouble sleeping, nightmares, anger, and anxiety.

CHAPTER SIX

THE AFTERMATH

For people impacted by Harvey, it was a relief when the storm finally passed. They had survived the worst. Now it was time to return home, assess the damage, and rebuild their lives. For many, this meant coming to terms with the scope of the recovery process. As Texas governor Greg Abbott said, "This is a place that Texas and FEMA [Federal Emergency Management Agency] will be involved in for a long, long time. We will be here until we can restore this region as back to normal as possible. . . . We need to recognize it's going to be a new normal."[1] FEMA administrator Brock Long agreed, saying, "[FEMA is] going to be here for several years helping [the region] recover."[2]

People began rebuilding as soon as they could after the hurricane.

WHO'S IN CHARGE?

Cities and counties have designated officials who manage relief and emergency responses. In Texas, emergency management directors develop emergency plans before a disaster, implement those plans during a disaster, and reassess and revise those plans after a disaster. During Harvey, disaster plans were implemented by emergency directors Rick Flanagan for the city of Houston, Judge Ed Emmett for Harris County, and Rick McLester for Aransas County along the Gulf of Mexico.

Harris County, where Houston is located, quickly posted a "Hurricane Harvey: Response and Responsibilities" chart on its website to explain which organizations were responsible for which recovery efforts after the storm. The chart details the specific roles of the US Army Corps of Engineers, FEMA, the Harris County Flood Control District, Harris County, and local cities and municipal utility districts. The county also shared contact information for all of the relevant organizations and teams involved in recovery. As part of this recovery, the Harris County Flood Control District partnered

FEMA tried to make it easy for Texas residents to apply for aid.

with the US Army Corps of Engineers, FEMA, the city of Houston, and the Harris County Engineering Department to address infrastructure repairs, debris removal, and maintenance. These partners also developed new flood damage reduction plans to improve the region's ability to withstand such powerful storms.

FEMA and private contractors began stepping in to rebuild homes, businesses, and infrastructure after Harvey. Certain public facilities were eligible for funding through FEMA's Public Assistance Grant Program, which matches contractors in prearranged emergency contracts with infrastructure needing repair or restoration. The company Strategic Partnerships also worked with contractors to

MORE TO THE STORY

UNDOCUMENTED WORKERS

It is not unprecedented for policies to become more flexible in the wake of huge disasters. After Hurricane Katrina, President George W. Bush relaxed workplace rules. For more than one month, employers did not have to verify that new employees were authorized to work in the United States. This allowed survivors to work while they waited for new identification documents to replace those lost during the storm. It also allowed undocumented workers, who have no documents at all, to get work. Undocumented workers made up approximately 25 percent of the construction workforce during the rebuild after Katrina.[3] They contributed valuable work toward the city's recovery.

Contractors argued for loosening laws again in the aftermath of Harvey. Texas had already been experiencing a severe labor shortage before the disaster. Given that approximately 15 percent of construction workers in the United States are unauthorized, it was hard to see how the region would be able to jump-start recovery without employing undocumented workers. As Scott Norman, executive director of the Texas Association of Builders, said, "We are going to need these people to try and rebuild parts of Texas that have been devastated."[4]

connect them with rebuilding opportunities throughout the state. Looking at the extent of the rebuild, Jeffrey Nielsen, the executive director of the Houston Contractors Association, noted that his team was going to be very busy.

Contractors had their own concerns during the post-Harvey rebuild, including finding enough construction workers. Both the Houston Contractors Association and the Greater Houston Builders Association had seen labor shortages even before the storm. Nielsen partly attributed these shortages to low interest in the work. An estimated one-third of Houston's civil construction workers were undocumented. But with Texas's strict immigration laws and President Donald Trump's tough immigration policies, those workers were increasingly

ILLEGITIMATE CONTRACTORS

After Harvey, not all contractors approaching hurricane victims were legitimate. Storm chaser contractors and other scammers targeted individuals who needed their homes or businesses rebuilt, offering quick turnarounds or too-good-to-be-true prices. Legitimate contractors can provide documents from the Institute of Inspection, Cleaning, and Restoration Certification, an international accreditation organization that develops certifications and standards for the cleaning, restoration, and inspection industries, as proof they adhere to an acceptable standard of work. They can also provide insurance and proof of their licensing.

deported or voluntarily left for more immigration-friendly states. US Immigration and Customs Enforcement had already made approximately 10,000 arrests in Houston under Trump's administration, the second-highest number in the country after Dallas, Texas.[5] With these labor shortages, the issue of finding workers to rebuild the region after Harvey increased the projected length of recovery.

IMMEDIATE NEEDS

After Harvey, individuals and families found themselves displaced and in need of immediate shelter. People with some savings could stay in a hotel, relocate to a mobile home park, set up a trailer beside their damaged house, or relocate out of the area. Others found temporary spots in nearby homeless shelters or churches with vacancies.

FEMA paid for tens of thousands of households to stay in hotel rooms or in apartments. But with the high demand for temporary housing, families were pushed farther and farther away from their neighborhoods and placed in hotels and apartments across the state. Making matters worse, Houston is a car-dependent city.

Shelters provided a safe space for thousands of people.

Estimates placed the number of cars destroyed in the flooding close to one million.[6] Without vehicles, people who ended up in temporary housing were far removed from many of the resources they needed. Others found housing through FEMA's partnership with prefabricated housing manufacturers, which produced thousands of homes after Harvey. But these families had to wait as the homes were delivered and installed.

Meanwhile, all of these people had to be fed. The Houston Food Bank, which has an average yearly output of 75 million pounds (34 million kg) of food, expected to distribute one million pounds (453,000 kg) of food each day. The food bank worked with the Texas Department of Agriculture and the US Department of Agriculture "to ensure available resources for a sustained response."[7]

CLEANUP

Before any rebuilding could occur, the city had to deal with the massive amounts of debris left by the storm. Individual survivors removed ruined furniture and debris from inside their homes, piling everything by the curb. They had two options for what to do next: pay a private company to move the debris or wait for the city to do it. The first option cost hundreds of dollars. The second took months.

A more dangerous type of cleanup also needed to happen. As the floodwaters receded, dampness in the floors, walls, and insulation of buildings contributed to mold. Aside from its awful smell, mold can give rise to bacteria and viruses, threatening residents' health. Professional companies offered a suite of post-flooding services. Companies offered services to prevent dampness from causing more extensive structural damage. They removed mold in a multistep process, filtering the air of mold spores, removing the mold and the porous surfaces in which mold grows, and ensuring the damaged areas remained thoroughly dry. But paying a professional company to clean and spray a house for mold can cost thousands of dollars, money that many survivors could not spare. As homeowners waited for insurance or public assistance to come in, the mold spread, decreasing the likelihood they could fully restore their homes.

MOLD IN RECOVERY

When buildings get water damage, the potential for mold is everywhere. Black mold is toxic and can lead to health problems. Because mold is a fungi, it can be hard to kill. It seeps into organic material and sends spores out into the air to find places to grow. The best way to kill mold is to get rid of what it is on or disinfect the area. Enough mold can cause structural damage to a building. This leads to many houses being condemned and torn down after large floods.

RISING TO THE OCCASION

Individuals and organizations stepped up to support victims and the rebuilding process. Sketch City, a group of local civic hackers—people who use technology and data to solve local issues—created a Google Maps–based website through which shelters and churches could identify their locations as well as their volunteer and donation needs. The group launched a similar map to coordinate cleanup after the floodwaters receded. People could

SKETCH CITY

Based in Houston, Sketch City is a nonprofit meet-up group of civic-minded entrepreneurs. The group's website describes its mission as advancing "technology and data in decisions that affect the public" and creating bots—software that performs simple tasks—and other technology to improve life in Houston.[9] Sketch City coordinated multiple efforts to promote communication for rescue and relief in the aftermath of Harvey. Past projects include a bot that tweets about air toxin levels and a map showing the frequency of parking tickets issued in different areas. Community members come together at monthly Civic Hack Nights to collaborate on computer coding projects to solve social issues. These issues can range from animal control to housing to criminal justice. Sketch City also hosts annual hackathons. In these events, developers, designers, and content experts form teams around specific civic issues—human trafficking, for example—and spend 24 hours brainstorming and implementing solutions using technology.

mark where they were located on the map and request help in mucking out and cleaning up their homes. Volunteers could also mark themselves on the map and provide their phone numbers, designating themselves as on-call for offering cleanup assistance.

In addition, the Texans, Houston's National Football League (NFL) team, brought in semitrucks filled with donated goods. Local entrepreneurs coordinated fund-raising and relief efforts. Hundreds of thousands of individuals donated to various funds developed in Harvey's wake, while corporations donated more than $150 million, according to the US Chamber of Commerce.[9] The American Red Cross raised $211 million.[8]

The Hurricane Harvey Relief Fund, launched by Emmett and Houston mayor Turner, focused on developing shelters and temporary housing, providing health care and transportation, and meeting childcare needs. The Rebuild Texas Fund, launched by Governor Abbott, focused on rebuilding small businesses, supporting the workforce, aiding schools and children, and meeting long-term needs in health and housing.

In addition, One America Appeal, an organization founded by former presidents Jimmy Carter, George H. W. Bush, Bill Clinton, George W. Bush, and Barack Obama, raised $31 million

DONATION FATIGUE

A common fund-raising concern is donation fatigue. Individuals and organizations often stop donating money as media attention around an issue dies down or moves on to the next disaster. Bob Ottenhoff, the CEO and president of the Center for Disaster Philanthropy, admitted that "the coverage kind of wears you out after a while."[10]

With Hurricanes Irma, which hit several islands in the Caribbean and Florida, and Maria, which devastated islands in the Caribbean including Puerto Rico, arriving soon after Harvey, major nonprofits saw a steep drop in fund-raising. The American Red Cross received $400 million in donations for Harvey, $56 million for Irma, and only $22 million for Maria. Drew Clark, the senior director of emergency funding for the nonprofit World Vision, further noted that "our fundraising has dropped off with each one of these successive disasters. We have seen some evidence of donor fatigue."[11]

Donation fatigue is one argument for finding a more sustainable solution to disaster recovery efforts. The outpouring of donations and volunteer support in the wake of catastrophes can be tremendous. But charity cannot always be guaranteed.

through concerts and ongoing donations by the end of October 2017.[12] In Texas, funds went to the Hurricane Harvey Relief Fund and Rebuild Texas Fund, which focused on rebuilding communities.

FEMA ON THE MOVE

FEMA's role immediately after the disaster was to find housing for victims, inspect damaged homes and businesses, and review assistance applications. FEMA put tens of thousands of people in hotels and provided rental assistance to others who could not return to damaged homes. Two months after Harvey, FEMA had inspected 249,952 properties for homeowners. FEMA had also inspected 235,946 properties for renters.[13]

FEMA's website provides up-to-date information on the assistance applications and dollars approved in the agency's various programs. Renters, homeowners, private nonprofits, and businesses could apply for a Small Business Administration (SBA) loan after Harvey. Those who did not

> "WE SPENT THE LAST TWO WEEKS JUST TEARING EVERYTHING OUT, TRYING TO SALVAGE WHAT WE CAN AND START THE REBUILDING PROCESS."[14]
>
> **— MITCH, A MAN WHOSE HOME WAS FLOODED AFTER HARVEY**

fall into these categories could submit an Other Needs Assistance application for expenses related to moving and storage, personal property damage, and costs of car repair or replacement. A Critical Needs Assistance fund provided a one-time payment for immediate needs, such as transportation, infant formula and diapers, prescriptions and other medical supplies, and food. Other specific grants covered the costs of childcare and medical or dental expenses directly related to Harvey.

The 2017 hurricane season continued after Harvey, and more disastrous hurricanes barreled into the Gulf of Mexico. As the areas recovered, discussions broke out about the role climate change played in the storms.

FROM THE HEADLINES

FOOTBALL PLAYER ORGANIZES RELIEF

Two days after Harvey hit, NFL player J. J. Watt took to Twitter. In a video posted on August 27, the Houston Texans defensive end said, "It's very difficult not only because [the football players] have family and friends back there . . . but that's our city. It's very tough to watch your city get hit by such a bad storm."[15] Watt launched a fund-raiser through the website YouCaring and encouraged fans to give what they could for Harvey relief.

Watt's original goal of raising $200,000 was accomplished in a mere two hours—and donations kept coming in. "The initial night, we broke the [YouCaring] site . . . and we somehow found the CEO's phone number and called him at his house and got him out of bed. He helped us fix the site and it got rolling,"

Watt said.[16] When total donations passed $6 million three days later, Watt raised the goal to $10 million.[17] With small individual donations and massive contributions by television shows and corporations, donors met and surpassed Watt's challenge. When the fund-raiser closed on September 15, a total of 209,315 donors had raised more than $37 million.[18]

Watt planned to reach out to experts who helped support victims after Katrina about the most effective way to use this money. In his final message to donors, Watt said, "When times are the toughest, humanity stands at its strongest and you have all helped to prove that emphatically. . . . Please keep this spirit of helping one another alive. The world is a better place when we all take care of each other."[19]

J. J. Watt, *right*, used the donation money to rebuild homes and provide food and medical services to victims of Harvey.

CHAPTER SEVEN

CLIMATE CHANGE AND NATURAL DISASTERS

The damage caused by Harvey left many wondering if the power and intensity of the hurricane was caused by climate change. For decades, human activity has produced more greenhouse gases. Instances of these activities include burning fossil fuels such as coal or oil to generate electricity. These greenhouse gases enter the atmosphere and make Earth warmer. When these gases are in the atmosphere, they decrease the amount of heat from the sun returning to space. This increases the overall temperature of Earth. This is called the greenhouse effect.

The effects of climate change are melting large amounts of ice each year.

PARIS AGREEMENT

Concerns about the greenhouse effect have spurred global action on climate change. On December 12, 2015, 195 countries in the United Nations adopted the Paris Agreement.[1] This was a formal agreement to lower greenhouse gas emissions around the world. The agreement set the goal of keeping the global temperature rise to less than 3.6 degrees Fahrenheit (2°C) during this century. The agreement was different from climate agreements of the past because it asked all countries to participate. In the past, the burden of lowering the effects of climate change had been put primarily on more developed countries. In 2017, President Trump announced that he would withdraw from the historic climate agreement. However, some cities and states in the United States have committed to upholding the terms of the accord.

Warming up the planet causes many different changes to the environment, including changes to weather patterns. Heat waves and droughts have become more frequent and so have floods and heavy rains.

Several environmental factors come together to form a hurricane. Many of these factors are affected by a warming planet. However, some of these factors, such as sea surface temperatures and wind shear, are also influenced by climate variations such as El Niño.

Scientists generally agree that there is no evidence of an increase in hurricane frequency globally due to climate change, although there is evidence of an increase in potential intensity of the strongest storms. Though organizations like NOAA cannot

NASA spacecraft help weather organizations predict accurate hurricane forecasts.

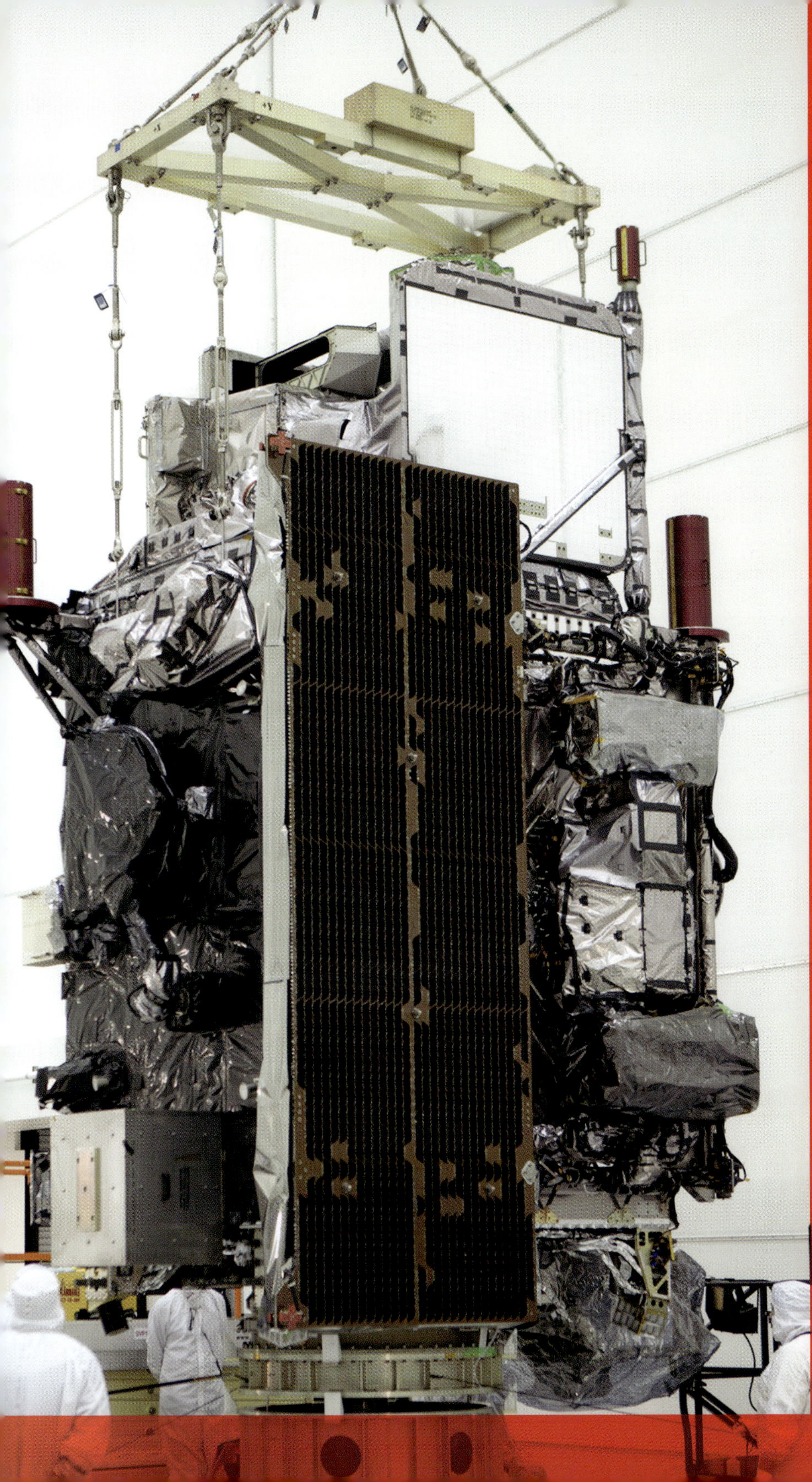

state definitively that climate change worsened Harvey, many are concerned for the future.

Harvey was not the only devastating hurricane to come out of the Atlantic basin in the 2017 hurricane season. Hurricane Irma struck the Caribbean and Florida in early September. That same month, Hurricane Maria devastated Puerto Rico and other islands in the Caribbean.

Hurricane Irma devastated some of the Caribbean islands.

While it's possible that the unusually high number of intense hurricanes in 2017 was just a temporary spike, it also may have been a response to climate change. After analyzing studies that predict the future impact of the greenhouse effect on hurricanes, NOAA reported that "it is likely that greenhouse warming will cause hurricanes in the coming century to be more intense globally and have higher rainfall rates than present-day hurricanes."[2] While Harvey may seem like a particularly powerful storm now, this kind of intensity may be the new norm.

"IN CONCLUSION, WHILE WE CANNOT SAY CLIMATE CHANGE 'CAUSED' HURRICANE HARVEY (THAT IS AN ILL-POSED QUESTION), WE CAN SAY THAT IT [WORSENED] SEVERAL CHARACTERISTICS OF THE STORM IN A WAY THAT GREATLY INCREASED THE RISK OF DAMAGE AND LOSS OF LIFE."[3]

— MICHAEL E. MANN, CLIMATOLOGIST

While the impacts of climate change on hurricane activity are somewhat uncertain, people can see the effects of climate change on the potential destruction caused by hurricanes. Rising temperatures cause sea ice to melt. Warming also causes the ocean water itself to expand. The result is rising sea levels, boosting the damage that storm surges can cause to coastal areas.

CLEAR
UNDO

WATER TEMPERATURE

Warm ocean water temperatures provide the conditions necessary for intense hurricanes to occur. When the temperature on the surface of the sea is warmer, convection is enhanced and more water evaporates. When this moisture in the atmosphere condenses, it fuels hurricanes.

Warm water from the Caribbean Sea moves into the Gulf of Mexico. Then, it goes back out to the Atlantic. This is called a loop current. On occasion, a few times a year, portions of it break off, called an eddy. The eddy moves through the western Gulf of Mexico. One of these was present as Harvey approached the coast of Texas, and this temperature spike caused

WHAT IS EL NIÑO?

El Niño refers to a weather pattern that occurs when ocean waters are unusually warm near the equator in the Pacific Ocean. It typically occurs every two to seven years and can last up to a year. El Niño can have a drastic effect on climate worldwide. El Niño–related temperature and precipitation impacts generally occur during the cold half of the year across the United States (October through March), when people tend to see wetter conditions around Florida and the Gulf Coast, and drier conditions along the Pacific Northwest and the Ohio Valley. During summer and fall, El Niño affects the atmospheric circulation in the North Atlantic Ocean and tends to suppress hurricane activity there.

The National Hurricane Center issues hurricane warnings.

Harvey to gain intensity. Harvey went from a tropical depression to a Category 4 hurricane in roughly 48 hours.

Historically, many hurricanes are not at their peak intensity while making landfall. But Harvey was, and that increased the devastation. If deep water below the hurricane is cold and is brought to the surface by the hurricane churning the water, this can cause the hurricane to become less intense. With Harvey, however, the water farther down in the ocean was still warm. The warm water caused Harvey to continue to intensify until it made landfall.

"CRAZY EVENTS KEEP HAPPENING. WE ARE SORT OF EXPECTING THEM, BUT WE STILL GET OVERWHELMED BECAUSE EXTREME WEATHER IS BY ITS NATURE PECULIAR AND JUST TOUGH TO PREDICT."[5]

— ADAM SOBEL, ATMOSPHERIC SCIENTIST

HARVEY'S RAINFALL AND CLIMATE CHANGE

As the air gets warmer, it can also hold approximately 7 percent more water for each degree Celsius increase.[4] This could cause larger, more intense hurricanes with more rainfall, though scientists are studying these links to gain a greater understanding of how hurricanes in the future will respond to such conditions.

Activists sometimes point to the impact of a warming planet on hurricanes when they demand action on climate change.

When Harvey hit Houston, it dropped a record-breaking amount of rain on the city. The US National Weather Service reported that a weather station near Houston measured approximately 52 inches (132 cm) of rain over the course of the storm.[6] This surpassed the previous record of 48 inches (122 cm), recorded in Medina, Texas—which is hundreds of miles west of Houston—during tropical storm Amelia in 1978.[7] Some climate scientists estimate that anywhere from 5 to 30 percent of Harvey's rainfall was caused by climate change.[8] However, these conditions cannot be directly attributed to the global warming trend. The vast floodwaters of warm water provided additional fuel for the hurricane.

PROPOSALS AFTER HARVEY

Harvey was one of the most expensive hurricanes in US history, with Governor Abbott predicting a full recovery would cost approximately $180 billion.[1] With this in mind, Congress met after the storm passed. Voting almost unanimously, the House of Representatives approved a $7.9 billion relief package on September 6, 2017.[2]

Senators rejected that proposal the following day, voting instead on a deal struck between President Trump and Democratic congressional leaders. This legislation provided $15.3 billion of relief aid and extended the National Flood Insurance Program.

Texas representatives Roger Williams, *left*, and Michael McCaul encouraged Congress to help with relief aid.

HOUSE OF
SENTATIVES

The Senate approved the legislation in an 80–17 vote.[3] Because legislation approved by one branch of Congress must also be approved by the other, the bill went back to the House for a vote. The House passed the bill on September 8. Most of this funding went to FEMA, with the rest used in the SBA disaster-loan program.

As funding came in for the victims of Harvey, officials continued to evaluate the damage. In particular, officials turned an analytical eye on Houston. They noted the disastrous impact that Harvey had on the city, and they began to look at ways to prevent such extensive damage in the future.

RECOVERY COST

The recovery for New Orleans after Hurricane Katrina cost an estimated $160 billion.[4] That was the record for the most in damages and recovery costs in the United States until Harvey hit Texas.

FUTURE OF HOUSTON

Harvey's floodwaters caused the Houston area to flood for the third year in a row. Philip Bedient, an environmental engineer, believed this would cause many politicians and their constituents to pursue policy changes in zoning

Former presidents attended a benefit concert to raise money for people impacted by the 2017 hurricane season.

and flood-prevention standards. Houston city officials let more expansion and development occur than the city could protect with out-of-date flood protection methods. The amount of flooding in Texas after Harvey brought formerly proposed ideas for how to protect the area back into consideration. Flooding will always be present in the Houston area due to its location, but experts note that managing and preventing rising waters must also be a part of the future development of the city. If measures aren't taken, Bedient says, "Houston is going to be forever known as the flood capital of the United States."[5]

After Harvey, recovery funds quickly started coming in for the area. As roads were repaved and utility lines were repaired, grant money allowed a great deal of work to be done in Houston. This work ensured utilities were more stable during winds and flooding, and more streets would have proper drainage systems.

Renovations in the days immediately following Harvey were straightforward. But it would be harder to continue to fight for renovations and improvements once life for the victims of Harvey had mostly returned to its normal rhythms. Bedient says the push for improvement

Volunteers helped clean out damaged homes.

AMAZING
SPIDER-MAN

would require more than code and zoning changes. He noted that Houston would need structural changes for drainage if it were to dodge such severe flooding in the future.

PREVENTING FUTURE DISASTROUS FLOODS

Many ideas have been proposed to the state legislature to keep Houston safe. Scientists from Rice University proposed the Mid-Bay Plan. This plan included a gate running across the Houston Ship Channel and a system of man-made reefs. The gate and reefs would keep commercial shipping safe during hurricanes by blocking storm surges and large waves. The plan would tie into a system of levees called a coastal spine that runs along the coast to protect communities around Galveston, Texas.

"IF WE REALLY ARE MOVING INTO A TIME OF GREATER DYNAMICS IN THE WEATHER—AND I THINK THE SCIENCE IS SUGGESTING THAT WE ARE—WE'RE GOING TO HAVE TO BUILD OUR CITIES DIFFERENTLY."[6]

— JEFF CARNEY, DIRECTOR OF THE COASTAL SUSTAINABILITY STUDIO—LOUISIANA STATE UNIVERSITY

Part of what made the flooding in Houston so bad was the amount of concrete used in the area. Increasing the space devoted to plants through parks, yards, and medians could help absorb water and reduce the amount of flooding caused by rain. New Orleans implemented similar plans after Katrina. The city created seven rain gardens for draining waters to absorb rainwater through plant life.

Experts note that one of the biggest changes Houston could make is to ban building in the 100-year floodplain, which is an area with a 1 out of 100 chance of flooding in a given year. Much of the recent growth in Houston has been in 100-year floodplains, which is something most cities don't allow. Also, existing developments in floodplains could be updated with features to force water into basins and rivers and away from buildings and streets. The current number of basins and bayous can't service the size and population of Houston with the amount of growth it has had. After Harvey, it was clear to some officials that Houston needed

SOIL ABSORPTION

The soil in the Houston metro area has heavy clay content. Because clay isn't permeable, it doesn't absorb water well. With all the clay in the soil in Houston, the water wasn't able to absorb into the ground as quickly as it could have in wetlands or forests.

Concrete is also not permeable and causes water to channel into areas that are already flooded. Houston also has a great deal of concrete in the city and the surrounding suburbs. During Harvey, this caused water to drain toward floodplains that were already full. When the water couldn't go anywhere, the concrete held the water like a big pool.

Texas governor Greg Abbott, *left*, continued to address safety concerns through initiatives after Harvey.

many more basins and bayous to remove water from the area.

Another change Houston could make is upgrading the protection to utilities and emergency services. If people had power, water, and food, then they could ride out floodwaters in higher floors rather than leaving town. Many died in floodwaters trying to escape Harvey. In addition, keeping emergency services such as hospitals and police stations operational is key. If hospitals could move patients to higher floors rather than sending them out of town, they could continue to help their communities. Functioning police stations keep people safe and deter looting.

Harvey left a great deal of destruction in Texas and the surrounding states. It crashed into Texas's coast as a Category 4 hurricane before stalling over the Houston area, bringing an abundance of rain and causing widespread flooding. After Harvey, relief aid came pouring in to help rebuild. Policy makers began to review options aimed at protecting the area from extensive damage in future storms. As they have in the wake of previous natural disasters, people will study Harvey and its impact to prepare for future hurricanes.

ESSENTIAL FACTS

MAJOR EVENTS

- On August 17, 2017, Harvey became a tropical storm in the Caribbean Sea and moved west. Less than one week later, Harvey hit the Gulf of Mexico and the warm water strengthened the storm. Harvey quickly became a Category 4 hurricane and made landfall on the Texas coast on August 25.
- Most of Harvey's damage was due to heavy rainfall. Flooding occurred in multiple states and caused destruction to homes and businesses.
- Houston experienced massive damage from Harvey. Much of this damage occurred due to Houston's layout and its position on a floodplain.
- After Harvey, Congress passed a $15.3 billion relief aid package.
- As of 2017, Harvey was the wettest hurricane on record for the United States.

KEY PLAYERS

- Sylvester Turner, the mayor of Houston, did not issue a mandatory evacuation order for the city. He believed a mass evacuation would cause more harm than good.
- Rescue teams helped injured or stranded people impacted by Harvey. They also assisted thousands of people in finding shelters.
- FEMA provided financial assistance to some people impacted by Harvey. The organization also helped rebuild businesses, homes, and infrastructure.
- Charity organizations such as One America Appeal raised money to help people affected by Harvey.

IMPACT ON SOCIETY

The damage caused by Harvey drastically impacted people's livelihood and the area's economy. However, the natural disaster also brought people together as they worked to rebuild the area.

QUOTE

"This will be a devastating disaster, probably the worst disaster the state's seen."

—William Long, FEMA administrator, predicting Harvey's significance two days after it hit land

GLOSSARY

BAYOU
A marshy area near a large body of water.

CLIMATE CHANGE
A series of effects caused by both natural and man-made contributions which influence long-term weather patterns.

COMBUSTIBLE
Easy to catch fire and burn.

CONTRACTOR
A person who signs a contract to manage a construction site, including overseeing the construction and managing the workers.

CONVECTION
The movement of a liquid or gas in which the cooler parts move down and the warmer parts rise.

ECOSYSTEM
A community of interacting organisms and their environment.

EYEWALL

A wall of clouds surrounding the eye of a hurricane; the eyewall contains the most damaging winds and intense rainfall.

GREENHOUSE GAS

A gas that absorbs infrared radiation and traps heat in the atmosphere.

INFLATION

An increase in the price of goods and services.

INFRASTRUCTURE

The physical structures, such as roads, railways, and power plants, that make it possible for a city or nation to function.

POVERTY

A socioeconomic state classified as being poor.

STORM SURGE

An abnormal rise in sea level during a storm, measured by how much higher it is than the normal level at whatever stage the tide is at.

WIND SHEAR

The difference in wind speed and/or direction between upper- and lower-level winds in the atmosphere.

ADDITIONAL RESOURCES

SELECTED BIBLIOGRAPHY

Collins, Jennifer and Paul Flaherty. "Keeping an 'Eye' on Tropical Research Data: The NOAA Hurricane Hunters, Their Missions and Their Recent Work with the University of South Florida to Archive Historical Information." *The Florida Geographer* 45 (2014): 14–27. Print.

Domonoske, Camila. "Why Didn't Officials Order the Evacuation of Houston?" *NPR*. NPR, 28 Aug. 2017. Web. 30 Oct. 2017.

Fischetti, Mark. "Hurricane Harvey: Why Is It So Extreme?" *Scientific American*. Scientific American, 28 Aug. 2017. Web. 30 Oct. 2017.

FURTHER READINGS

Bow, James. *Earth's Climate Change*. New York: Crabtree, 2016. Print.

Brown, Don. *Drowned City: Hurricane Katrina & New Orleans*. New York: Houghton Mifflin Harcourt, 2015. Print.

Willett, Edward. *Hurricane Irma*. Minneapolis: Abdo, 2018. Print.

ONLINE RESOURCES

Booklinks
NONFICTION NETWORK
FREE! ONLINE NONFICTION RESOURCES

To learn more about Hurricane Harvey, visit **abdobooklinks.com**. These links are routinely monitored and updated to provide the most current information available.

MORE INFORMATION

For more information on this subject, contact or visit the following organizations:

Federal Emergency Management Agency
500 C Street SW
Washington, DC 20472
202-646-2500
fema.gov
This agency provides up-to-date information on natural disasters occurring in the United States.

National Hurricane Center
11691 SW Seventeenth Street
Miami, FL 33165
305-229-4404
nhc.noaa.gov
This site tracks current storm disturbances and provides information about forecasts.

SOURCE NOTES

CHAPTER 1. A FLOODED CITY

1. "Harvey, Now a Tropical Storm, Carves a Path of Destruction Through Texas." *New York Times*. New York Times Company, n.d. Web. 30 Nov. 2017.
2. Karin Brulliard. "Harvey Is Also Displacing Wildlife." *Chicago Tribune*. Chicago Tribune, 28 Aug. 2017. Web. 30 Nov. 2017.
3. Andrew Freedman. "Historic, Catastrophic Flooding Underway in Houston from Tropical Storm Harvey." *Mashable*. Mashable, 27 Aug. 2017. Web. 30 Nov. 2017.
4. Mallory Simon. "Path of Destruction: What Hurricane Harvey Left in Its Wake." *CNN*. Cable News Network, 5 Sept. 2016. Web. 30 Nov. 2017.
5. "Houston City, Texas." *United States Census Bureau*. United States Census Bureau, n.d. Web. 30 Nov. 2017.
6. "The Wrath of Hurricane Harvey." *CBS*. CBS Interactive, 3 Sept. 2017. Web. 30 Nov. 2017.
7. Camila Domonoske. "Why Didn't Officials Order the Evacuation of Houston?" *NPR*. NPR, 28 Aug. 2017. Web. 30 Nov. 2017.
8. Tim Craig. "The Mayor of Corpus Christi Knows the Power Of Water, And It Guides His Decisions." *Washington Post*. Washington Post, 27 Aug. 2017. Web. 30 Nov. 2017.
9. Kalhan Rosenblatt. "Houston Officials Defend Not Ordering Hurricane Harvey Evacuation." *NBC*. NBC, 28 Aug. 2017. Web. 30 Nov. 2017.
10. "Houston City, Texas." *United States Census Bureau*. United States Census Bureau, n.d. Web. 30 Nov. 2017.
11. "Houston Area Economic Summary." *Bureau of Labor Statistics*. U.S. Department of Labor, n.d. Web. 30 Nov. 2017.
12. Rick Jervis and John Bacon. "'A Very Heavy Lift:' Harvey Will Drive 30,000 to Shelters in Texas, FEMA says." *USA Today*. USA Today, 28 Aug. 2017. Web. 30 Nov. 2017.

CHAPTER 2. HOW A HURRICANE FORMS

1. Joseph A. Zehnder. "Tropical Cyclone." *Encyclopedia Britannica*. Encyclopedia Britannica, n.d. Web. 30 Nov. 2017.
2. Ibid.
3. Ibid.
4. Chris Dolce. "The Storm That Killed 300,000." *Weather Channel*. Weather Company, 25 Apr. 2014. Web. 30 Nov. 2017.
5. Michael Snyder. "18 Startling Quotes about the Incredible Destruction Caused by Hurricane Sandy." *Economic Collapse*. Economic Collapse, 30 Oct. 2012. Web. 30 Nov. 2017.
6. "Saffir-Simpson Hurricane Wind Scale." *National Hurricane Center*. US Department of Commerce, n.d. Web. 30 Nov. 2017.
7. Ibid.
8. Ibid.
9. Ibid.

10. Ibid.
11. Ibid.
12. Tim Newcomb. "Quote: Forecasting Hurricanes Not an Exact Science." *Time*. Time, 31 Aug. 2011. Web. 30 Nov. 2017.

CHAPTER 3. HARVEY'S ARRIVAL

1. "Historic Hurricane Harvey's Recap." *Weather Channel*. Weather Company, 2 Sept. 2017. Web. 30 Nov. 2017.
2. Ibid.
3. "Major Hurricane Harvey—August 25–29, 2017." *National Weather Service*. US Department of Commerce, n.d. Web. 30 Nov. 2017.
4. Mark Fischetti. "Hurricane Harvey: Why Is It So Extreme?" *Scientific American*. Scientific American, 28 Aug. 2017. Web. 30 Nov. 2017.
5. "Major Hurricane Harvey—August 25–29, 2017." *National Weather Service*. US Department of Commerce, n.d. Web. 30 Nov. 2017.
6. Joel Achenback and Lisa Rein. "FEMA Director Says Harvey Is Probably the Worst Disaster in Texas History." *Washington Post*. Washington Post, 27 Aug. 2017. Web. 30 Nov. 2017.
7. Jason Samenow. "Harvey Is A 1,000 Year Flood Event Unprecedented in Scale." *Washington Post*. Washington Post, 31 Aug. 2017. Web. 30 Nov. 2017.
8. "Historic Hurricane Harvey's Recap." *Weather Channel*. Weather Company, 2 Sept. 2017. Web. 30 Nov. 2017.
9. Karin Brulliard. "How the Chaos of Hurricane Katrina Helped Save Pets from Flooding in Texas." *Denver Post*. Digital First Media, 31 Aug. 2017. Web. 30 Nov. 2017.

CHAPTER 4. DESTRUCTION IN HOUSTON

1. "About Houston." *City of Houston*. City of Houston, n.d. Web. 30 Nov. 2017.
2. Kim McGuire. "Houston's Development Boom and Reduction of Wetlands Leave Region Flood Prone." *Houston Chronicle*. Hearst Newspapers, 22 July 2016. Web. 30 Nov. 2017.
3. Jon Erdman. "Is Houston America's Flood Capital?" *Weather Channel*. Weather Company, 24 Aug. 2017. Web. 30 Nov. 2017.
4. Rod Pinheiro. "Storm Water Maintenance Branch." *City of Houston*. City of Houston, n.d. Web. 30 Nov. 2017.
5. Adam M. Zaretsky. "After the 500-Year Flood: an Early Look at the Return to Normalcy." *Federal Reserve Bank of St. Louis*. Federal Reserve, n.d. Web. 30 Nov. 2017.
6. Neena Satija and Kiah Collier. "Houston's 'Flood Czar' Says Harvey Has Brought the City to a Decision Point on Flood Control." *Texas Tribune*. Texas Tribune, 13 Sept. 2017. Web. 30 Nov. 2017.
7. Thom Patterson. "How Houston's Layout May Have Made Its Flooding Worse." *CNN*. Cable News Network, 31 Aug. 2017. Web. 30 Nov. 2017.
8. "By the Numbers: Hurricane Harvey Hits 6 Million Texans with 30+ Inches of Rain." *ABC*. ABC, 2 Sept. 2017. Web. 30 Nov. 2017.
9. Dylan Baddour, Kevin Sullivan, Wesley Lowery, and Robert Samuels. "Harvey Drops Nearly Two Feet of Water on Houston Area, Causing Deadly Floods." *Post and Courier*. Post and Courier, 27 Aug. 2017. Web. 30 Nov. 2017.
10. "Houston Flooded by Tropical Storm Harvey." *YouTube*. YouTube, 28 Aug. 2017. Web. 30 Nov. 2017.
11. Konrad Putzier. "Hurricane Harvey Put as Much as $55 Billion Worth of Houston's Commercial Real Estate Underwater." *Business Insider*. Business Insider, 2 Sept. 2017. Web. 30 Nov. 2017.
12. Melissa Jeltsen and Andy Campbell. "This Pilot Rescued More People in Harvey Than in the Rest of His Career Combined." *Huffpost*. Oath, 2 Sept. 2017. Web. 30 Nov. 2017.
13. Adam Rogers. "With Harvey, Imperfect Engineering Meets a Perfect Storm." *Wired*. Condé Nast, 31 Aug. 2017. Web. 30 Nov. 2017.
14. Travis Fedschun. "Harvey Floodwaters Overflow Houston Reservoir, Separate Levee Breach Reported." *Fox News*. Fox News Network, 29 Aug. 2017. Web. 30 Nov. 2017.

SOURCE NOTES CONTINUED

CHAPTER 5. HARVEY'S IMPACT

1. J. J. Gallagher. "Hurricane Harvey Wreaks Historic Devastation: by the Numbers." *ABC.* ABC News Internet Ventures, 1 Sept. 2017. Web. 30 Nov. 2017.

2. Colin Dwyer. "'The Goal Is Rescue:' The Massive Response to Harvey, by the Numbers." *NPR.* NPR, 28 Aug. 2017. Web. 30 Nov. 2017.

3. Stephanie Elam. "Parts of Texas Still in Rescue and Recovery Mode, 2 Weeks after Hurricane Harvey." *CNN.* Cable News Network, 8 Sept. 2017. Web. 30 Nov. 2017.

4. Jen Christensen. "After 60 Years of Helping Beaumont, Texas Hospital Needed Help of Its Own." *CNN.* Cable News Network, 1 Sept. 2017. Web. 30 Nov. 2017.

5. Giulia Afiune. "State Says Harvey's Death Toll Has Reached 88." *Texas Tribune.* Texas Tribune, 13 Oct. 2017. Web. 30 Nov. 2017.

6. Matt Egan and Betsy Klein. "Trump Taps Emergency U.S. Oil Reserve after Harvey." *CNN.* Cable News Network, 31 Aug. 2017. Web. 30 Nov. 2017.

CHAPTER 6. THE AFTERMATH

1. "Transcripts." *CNN.* Cable News Network, n.d. Web. 30 Nov. 2017.

2. "William B. 'Brock' Long." *FEMA.* Department of Homeland Security, n.d. Web. 30 Nov. 2017.

3. Alexia Fernández Campbell. "All the Relief Money in the World Won't Rebuild Houston. Undocumented Workers Will." *Vox.* Vox Media, 7 Sept. 2017. Web. 30 Nov. 2017.

4. Jonathan Berr. "Will Houston Find Enough Workers to Rebuild after Harvey?" *CBS.* CBS Interactive, 31 Aug. 2017. Web. 1 Dec. 2017.

5. Elliot Spagat. "Labor Shortage Impedes Harvey Recovery." *Mercury News.* Digital First Media, 5 Sept. 2017. Web. 30 Nov. 2017.

6. Alex Davis. "Harvey Wrecks Up To a Million Cars in Car-Dependent Houston." *Wired.* Condé Nast, 3 Sept. 2017. Web. 30 Nov. 2017.

7. "Rebuilding Lives after Harvey, Irma, Jose and Maria." *News on Weather.* News on Weather, 16 Oct. 2017. Web. 30 Nov. 2017.

8. Melissa Chan. "How the Kindness of Strangers Is Helping Hurricane Victims Rebuild Their Lives." *Time.* Time, 14 Sept. 2017. Web. 30 Nov. 2017.

9. "Advancing Technology and Data in Decision That Affect the Public." *Sketch City.* Sketch City, n.d. Web. 1 Dec. 2017.

10. Andy Segedin and Mark Hrywna. "Rebuilding Lives after Harvey, Irma, Jose and Maria." *NonProfit Times.* NonProfit Times Publishing Group, 16 Oct. 2017. Web. 1 Dec. 2017.

11. "Hurricanes Produce Donor Fatigue." *Reuters.* Reuters, 13 Oct. 2017. Web. 1 Dec. 2017.

12. Caroline Kenny and Allie Malloy. "5 Ex-Presidents Attend Hurricane Relief Concert; Trump Appears in Video Message." *CNN.* Cable News Network, 22 Oct. 2017. Web. 30 Nov. 2017.

13. "Ensuring an Equitable Recovery for Renters Impacted by Hurricane Harvey." *National Low Income Housing Coalition*. National Low Income Housing Coalition, 31 Oct. 2017. Web. 30 Nov. 2017.

14. Tom Dart. "Houston after Harvey: City Faces Huge Hurdle to Recovery." *Guardian*. Guardian News and Media Limited, 25 Sept. 2017. Web. 1 Dec. 2017.

15. JJ Watt (JJWatt). "Recovery Efforts from Hurricane Harvey Will Be Massive. 27 Aug. 2017. 2:28 PM. Tweet.

16. Leinz Vales. "J.J. Watt Keeps Surpassing Harvey Relief Goal: 'I'm with Them for the Long Haul.'" *CNN*. Cable News Network, 1 Sept. 2017. Web. 1 Dec. 2017.

17. John Bonazzo. "J.J. Watt, Houston Texas Raise Over $6 Million for Harvey Relief on YouCaring." *Observer*. Observer, 30 Aug. 2017. Web. 1 Dec. 2017.

18. "Houston Flood Relief Fund." *YouCaring*. YouCaring, n.d. Web. 1 Dec. 2017.

19. Ibid.

CHAPTER 7. CLIMATE CHANGE AND NATURAL DISASTERS

1. Coral Davenport. "Nations Approve Landmark Climate Accord in Paris." *New York Times*. New York Times Company, 12 Dec. 2015. Web. 1 Dec. 2017.

2. "Global Warming and Hurricanes." *GFDL*. US Department of Commerce, n.d. Web. 1 Dec. 2017.

3. German Lopez. "How Global Warming Likely Made Harvey Much Worse, Explained by a Climatologist." *Vox*. Vox Media, 28 Aug. 2017. Web. 1 Dec. 2017.

4. Umair Irfan. "One of the Clearest Signs of Climate Change in Hurricanes Maria, Irma, and Harvey Was the Rain." *Vox*. Vox Media, 29 Sept. 2017. Web. 1 Dec. 2017.

5. Eliza Barclay. "Harvey Is Part of a Pattern of Extreme Weather Scientists Saw Coming. They're Still Shocked." *Vox*. Vox Media, 31 Aug. 2017. Web. 1 Dec. 2017.

6. "Storm Summary Message." *Weather Prediction Center*. US Department of Commerce, n.d. Web. 1 Dec. 2017.

7. US National Weather Service (NWS). "Preliminary Data from at Least One Texas Rain Gauge Appears to Have Broken the Texas Tropical Cyclone Rainfall Record." *Facebook*. Facebook, 29 Aug. 2017. Web. 1 Dec. 2017.

8. Eliza Barclay. "Harvey Is Part of a Pattern of Extreme Weather Scientists Saw Coming. They're Still Shocked." *Vox*. Vox Media, 31 Aug. 2017. Web. 1 Dec. 2017.

CHAPTER 8. PROPOSALS AFTER HARVEY

1. Jeffrey Kluger. "Houston after Harvey." *Time*. Time, 7 Sept. 2017. Web. 1 Dec. 2017.

2. Ashley Killough, Deirdre Walsh, and Ted Barrett. "House Passes Hurricane Harvey Relief Aid." *CNN*. Cable News Network, 6 Sept. 2017. Web. 1 Dec. 2017.

3. Thomas Kaplan. "Senate Votes to Raise Debt Limit and Approves $15 Billion in Hurricane Relief." *New York Times*. New York Times Company, 7 Sept. 2017. Web. 1 Dec. 2017.

4. Nathanael Johnson. "The U.S. Should Go Dutch to Avoid Building Another Houston." *Grist*. Grist Magazine, 31 Aug. 2017. Web. 1 Dec. 2017.

5. Diane Toomey. "As Harvey's Floodwaters Recede, How Should Houston Rebuild?" *Yale Environment 360*. Yale School of Forestry & Environmental Studies, 5 Sept. 2017. Web. 1 Dec. 2017.

6. Nathanael Johnson. "The U.S. Should Go Dutch to Avoid Building Another Houston." *Grist*. Grist Magazine, 31 Aug. 2017. Web. 1 Dec. 2017.

INDEX

ABOUT THE AUTHOR

Cliff Waterford is a nonfiction children's book writer. He lives in Minnesota.